www.herdthinners.com

Kevin & Kell: Seen Anything Unusual? is an original publication of Online Features Syndicate and is published in conjunction with Plan Nine Publlshing.

Second Printing September 1999
ISBN 0-9660676-1-4

Online Features Syndicate
P.O. Box 931264
Norcross, GA 30093

Printed in the USA.

Thanks to David Allen and the whole
gang at Plan Nine.

And lastly, thanks to my partner Doug Pratt, who had an idea
for marketing a comic strip in cyberspace!

PLAN NINE
PUBLISHING

2 Salem St. Suite 314
Thomasville, NC 27360
(336) 472-6463
www.plan9.org

*Bringing you the future tomorrow,
but what's funny today!*

MEET THE DEWCLAWS

AND THEIR FRIENDS...

KELL
A WOLF, AND A STAFF PREDATOR AT HERD THINNERS, INC.

LINDESFARNE
A TEENAGE PORCUPINE, ADOPTED DURING KEVIN'S FIRST MARRIAGE

CONEY
KEVIN AND KELL'S DAUGHTER, A CARNIVOROUS BUNNY

KEVIN
A RABBIT, AND THE SYSOP OF THE ONLINE HERBIVORE FORUM

RUDY
AN EARLY TEEN WOLF CUB, KELL'S SON FROM A PREVIOUS MARRIAGE

Candace

Fenton

Bruno (and Corrie)

Fiona Fennec (And her parents)

The Ursals

Ms. Aura

Ralph

5

6

7

8

9

10

11

14

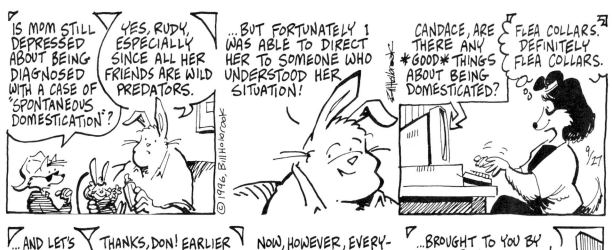

15

16

17

19

20

22

23

24

25

26

10/31

27

28

POOR RUDY! HE AND FIONA ARE SO CLOSE... BUT UNABLE TO COMMUNICATE!

I'M SURE THE FRUSTRATION IS INCREDIBLE.

...BUT AT LEAST THEY'VE BEEN ABLE TO CHANNEL IT PRODUCTIVELY!

WHAT A TURNAROUND! ANOTHER "A"!

CAN I GO DO SOME MORE EXTRA CREDIT?

© 1996, Bill Holbrook

THIS IS TRAGIC! RUDY AND FIONA ARE FINALLY REUNITED, AND FIND THEY CAN ONLY COMMUNICATE ONLINE!

THEY'RE DOOMED TO A DISTANT, NON-PHYSICAL RELATIONSHIP!

© 1996, Bill Holbrook

WORKS FOR ME.

I'M COOL.

PARENTS.

SO YOU'VE FOUND THAT AFTER BEING APART, YOU CAN ONLY TALK TO EACH OTHER ONLINE?

NOD · NOD

HMM... THERE MUST BE **SOME** OTHER FORM OF COMMUNICATION THAT YOU HAVE IN COMMON... HEY! I KNOW!

11/8

THEY'RE ON HOLD TO TECH SUPPORT TOGETHER.

©1996, Bill Holbrook

EVEN THOUGH WE CAN ONLY COMMUNICATE ONLINE, WE CAN STILL GO ON DATES, FIONA!

HOW, RUDY?

ALL WE'RE ABLE TO DO IS SIT IN THE MOONLIGHT WHILE STARING AT A SCREEN!

11/11

EVER HEARD OF SOMETHING CALLED "DRIVE-IN MOVIES"?

NO, WHY?

©1996, Bill Holbrook

31

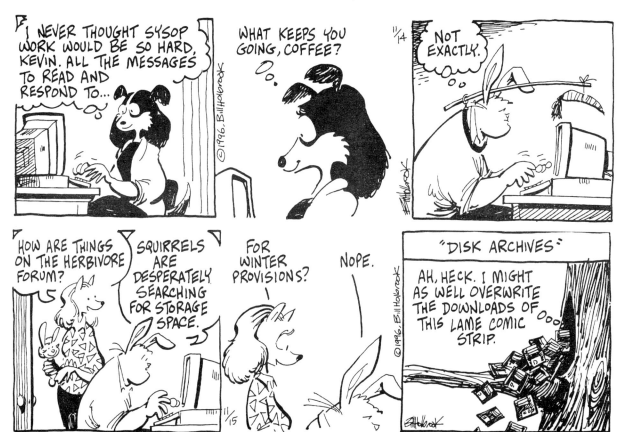

32

33

34

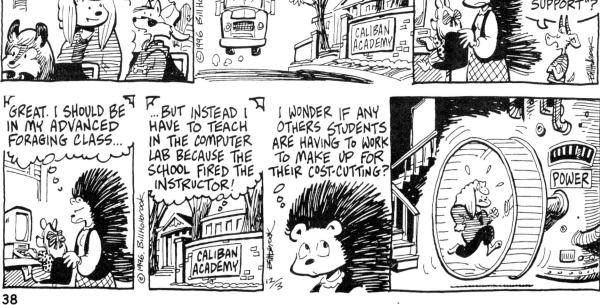

40

41

42

43

44

46

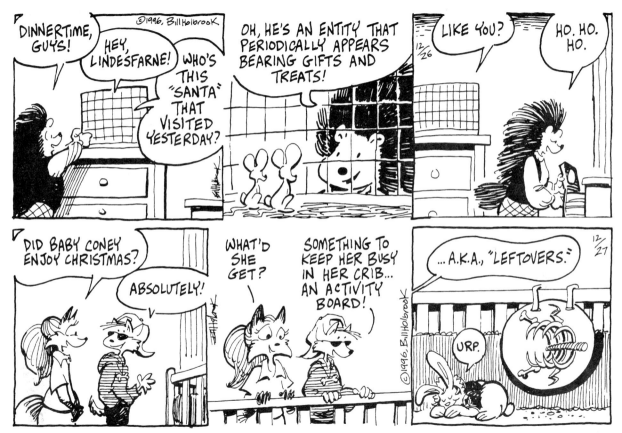

47

49

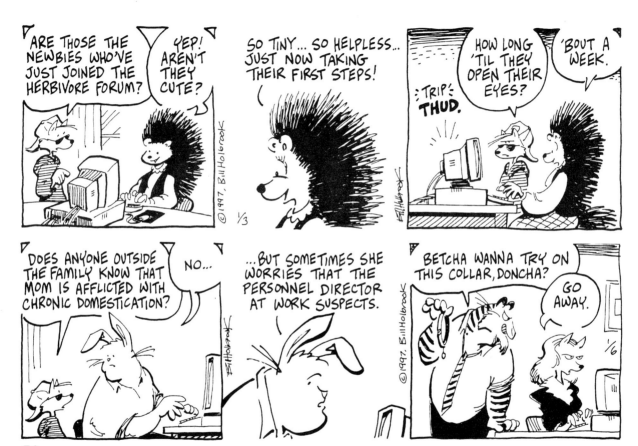

50

52

54

55

56

57

58

60

2/4

PEEL

THE WALLPAPER CAME OFF MY WEB SITE.

I TOLD YOU TO USE MORE PASTE.

YES, MOTHER, WHEN RUDY WAS A BABY THE HOLES IN HIS BOTTLE NIPPLES KEPT GETTING CLOGGED UP.

BUT **NOW**, THAT'S NEVER A PROBLEM!

2/5

62

63

67

69

71

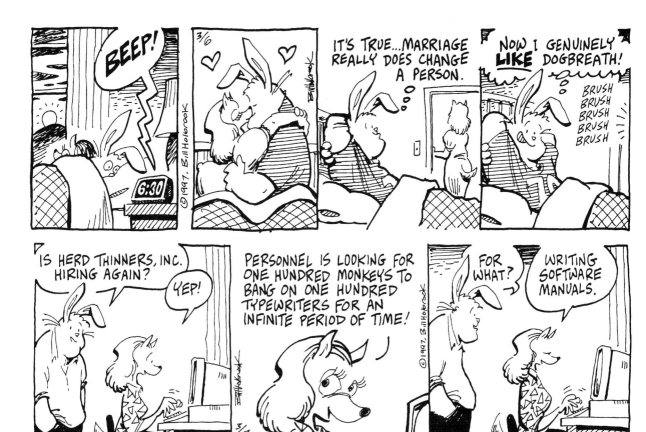

3/10

© 1997, Bill Holbrook

73

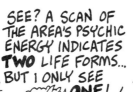

78

THERE MUST BE **FIVE** THOUSAND OUT THERE TODAY!

BUT I'VE HEALED EVERY MACHINE IN TOWN! THERE'S NOTHING LEFT TO FIX!

BEEP!

POINK!

4/3

...EXCEPT THAT?

I'M TRYING! I'M TRYING!

EVER SINCE THAT TAG FELL OFF YOUR EAR, THINGS HAVE GONE BACK TO NORMAL PRETTY QUICKLY.

FIONA LOSES POWERS

NO MORE CROWDS! NO MORE ZEALOTS! NO MORE FANATICAL WORSHIPPERS ALWAYS BOTHERING YOU! YOU'RE JUST GOOD OL' ⸱OOF!⸱ FIONA!

ZAP.

TINK!

DISAPPOINTED?

NOT REALLY.

4/4

FIONA LOSES POWERS

84

I'M GLAD YOU COULD COME BY, CANDACE. I'M MAKING SOME CHANGES IN THE HERBIVORE FORUM.

YES, OUR MEMBERSHIP **HAS** GOTTEN STAGNANT...

EXACTLY! SO I'M OPENING UP A NEW SECTION!

FOR WHAT?

OMNIVORES.

HOW ARE YOU AT HERDING BEARS?

SAY, CORRIE... YOU DON'T TALK ABOUT YOUR FAMILY MUCH...

© 1997, BillHolbrook

DO YOU HAVE ANY RELATIVES?

WELL...

NOW I DO...

SHEEP CLONED

85

86

90

91

92

94

95

98

99

100

102

103

104

105

108

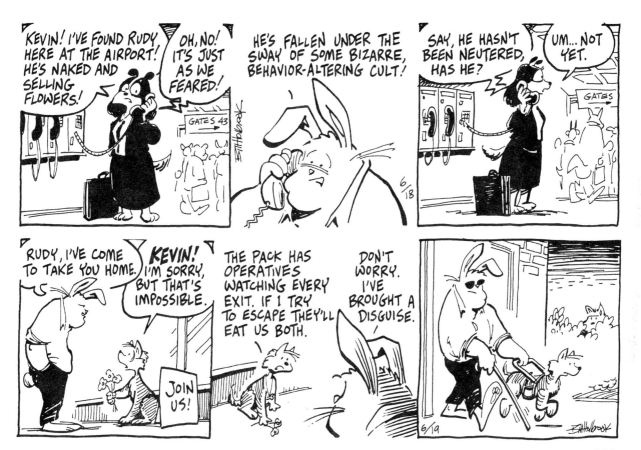

109

110

111

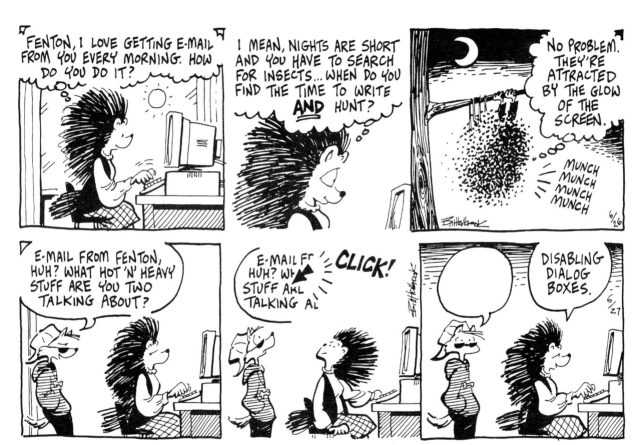

112

116

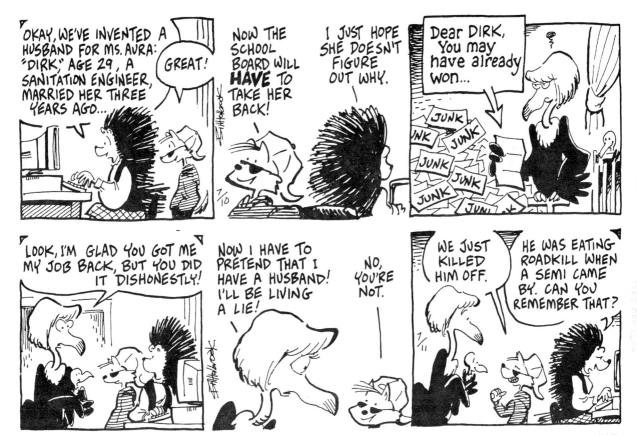

121

WHEN ONE IS MARRIED, IT'S NATURAL FOR CERTAIN BEHAVIORS TO RUB OFF.

PRACTICES CAN BE ADOPTED WITHOUT EVEN REALIZING IT.

7/28

NEW TROPHY, DAD?

YEAH, I HAD IT STUFFED AND MOUNTED.

KEVIN, MAY I BORROW YOUR LAPTOP?

CERTAINLY, KELL!

I'LL JUST PERSONALIZE IT FOR YOU.

THANKS!

7/29

123

PAST PRESIDENTS OF HERD THINNERS, INC.

7/30

QUIT LAUGHING AND GET ME DOWN, OKAY?

SNORT

7/31

124

125

126

128

129

131

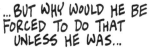

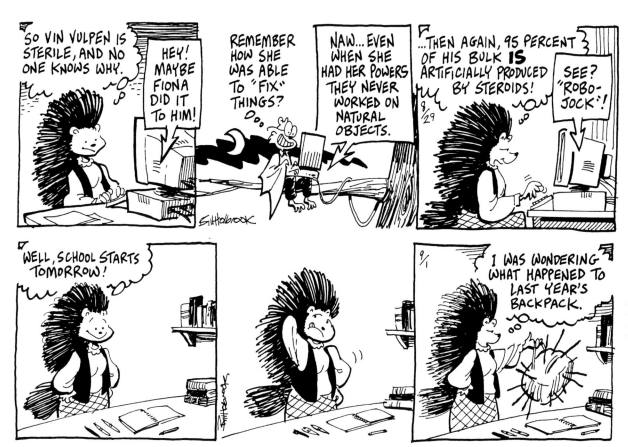

135

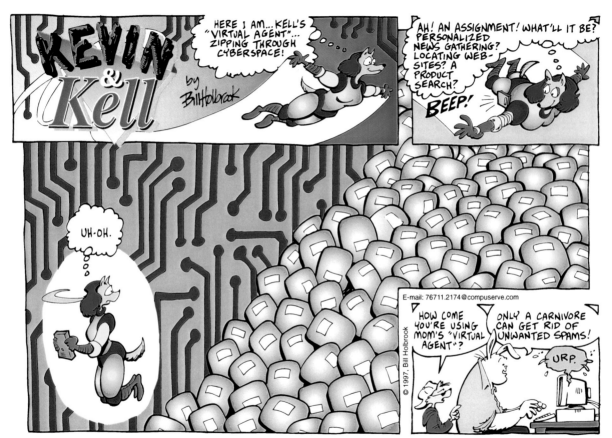

136

Kevin & Kell by Bill Holbrook

E mail: 76711.2174@compuserve.com

I UPGRADED OUR SYSTEM! WHAT DO YOU THINK?

COOL!

See a new "Kevin & Kell" strip every weekday at http://ourworld.compuserve.com/homepages/chris_galvin/kevkel.html or on CompuServe at GO FUNFOR

SHREAD RIP MANGLE Tear SUNDER

UNFORTUNATELY, THE COMPUTER VIRUSES THOUGHT IT WAS A SCRATCHING POST.

BAD! BAD! BAD! BAD!

© 1997, Bill Holbrook

137

See "Kevin & Kell" every weekday at http://ourworld.compuserve.com/homepages/chris_galvin/kevkel.html

© 1997 Bill Holbrook

Email: 76711.2174@compuserve.com

© 1996, Bill Holbrook

139

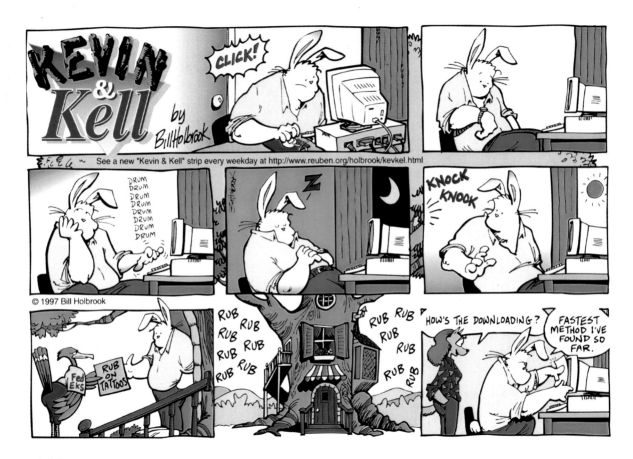

140